Arrowwood Elementary School
10345 Arrowwood Drive
Highlands Ranch, CO 80126

DATE DUE

GAYLORD			PRINTED IN U.S.A.

AWESOME ATHLETES

VENUS & SERENA WILLIAMS

Lydia Pyle

ABDO Publishing Company

visit us at
www.abdopub.com

Published by ABDO Publishing Company, 4940 Viking Drive, Edina, Minnesota 55435.
Copyright © 2004 by Abdo Consulting Group, Inc. International copyrights reserved in all
countries. No part of this book may be reproduced in any form without written permission from
the publisher.

Printed in the United States.

Cover Photo: Corbis
Interior Photos: Corbis pp. 12, 15, 17, 19; Getty Images pp. 7, 20, 21, 23, 25, 27; *Sports
  Illustrated* pp. 5, 8, 9, 11, 13, 14, 15, 22, 29, 30, 31

Editor: Tamara L. Britton and Jessica A. Klein
Art Direction: Jessica A. Klein

Library of Congress Cataloging-in-Publication Data

Pyle, Lydia, 1972-
    Venus and Serena Williams / Lydia Pyle.
        p. cm. -- (Awesome athletes)
    Includes index.
    Summary: Describes the lives and careers of the two African American sisters who have had
sensational success in the world of professional tennis.
    ISBN 1-59197-486-0
    1. Williams, Venus, 1980---Juvenile literature. 2. Williams, Serena, 1981---Juvenile literature.
3. Tennis players--United States--Biography--Juvenile literature. 4. African American women
tennis players--Biography--Juvenile literature. [1. Williams, Venus, 1980- 2. Williams, Serena,
1981- 3. Tennis players. 4. African Americans--Biography. 5. Women--Biography.] I. Title. II.
Series.

GV994.A1P95 2003
796.342'092'2--dc21
    [B]   2003045398

Contents

The Williams Sisters

In 1998, Venus and Serena Williams played against each other for the first time in a **professional** tournament. The sisters began what has become an awesome rivalry in the tennis world. That rivalry continues today.

Together Venus and Serena have won nine Grand Slam singles tournaments. Serena has won five and Venus has won four. Venus is older than Serena by 15 months, so she began playing tennis first. Venus rose to the top of women's tennis before Serena. However, in the last few years Serena has pulled ahead in the game.

When these sisters began playing tennis at the age of four, their dad knew they had talent. With hard work and dedication, they have dominated the courts. Their amazing athletic ability, quick speed, and sure power have made women's tennis one of today's most popular spectator sports.

Venus (r) and Serena pose at the net.

Family Life

Richard and Oracene Williams were blessed with daughters. They already had three—Lyndrea, Isha, and Yetunde—when Venus Ebone Starr was born on June 17, 1980. Fifteen months later, on September 26, 1981, Serena was born.

Richard moved the family to an inner-city area of Compton, California, shortly after Serena was born. The Williamses could afford to live in a better area, but Richard wanted his girls to grow up in a tough neighborhood. He thought this would better prepare them for the world.

Richard once saw a tennis tournament on television. The winner won $30,000. It was at that moment that he decided his girls were going to play tennis. He watched tennis videos and educated himself about the game. As each daughter turned four years old, he brought her out on the tennis court and had her hit balls. Neither Lyndrea, Isha, or Yetunde took to the game.

Venus and her sister Lyndrea

But when Richard took Venus out on the court, she immediately loved the game. She hit hundreds of balls and showed great promise. Serena was the same way.

The public tennis courts in Compton were less than perfect. They were old and cracked, and graffiti was everywhere. Gangs hung around the court and gunfire was often heard. Still, Richard had the girls out there practicing all the time.

Venus (l) and Serena share a strong bond.

Tennis wasn't the only important thing in the girls' lives. There was also school. If the girls didn't do well in school, they did not get to play tennis. So they worked hard, both in school and at tennis.

Richard teaches Venus how to serve.

Growing Up

Soon, Venus and Serena were playing in local tournaments and winning. They were also playing junior tournaments, which were **sanctioned** by the United States Tennis Association (USTA).

Richard limited the number of tournaments the girls were allowed to play in. He did not want them to burn out or get injured. By the time Venus was 12 and Serena was 11, they had won most of their tennis matches. Venus had a record of 63-0, and Serena's record was 46-3. The girls were becoming well known in the junior tennis world.

Then, Richard did something that many people questioned. He pulled the girls off the junior circuit. He didn't want his daughters to feel the pressure of winning on the junior circuit. He also wanted them to concentrate on school and take up other interests. The girls still practiced tennis, but they didn't compete in tournaments.

In 1991, Richard moved the family to Palm Beach Gardens, Florida, so that Venus and Serena could attend a tennis academy run by Ric Macci. Macci had worked with Jennifer Capriati and Mary Pierce. When the girls weren't training, they attended Carver Middle School. Then in 1993, the girls were homeschooled for a time. Both girls later graduated from the Driftwood Academy, a private, 30-student high school.

Venus (r) and Serena compete in a doubles tournament.

Rising Stars

On October 31, 1994, Venus turned pro. She made her **professional** debut at the Bank of the West Classic in Oakland, California. The next year, Serena turned pro. Her first tournament was the Bell Challenge in Quebec City, Canada. Both girls only played in a few tournaments their first couple of years as professionals. They did not have much success.

In 1997, Venus played in her first Grand Slam event, the French Open. That same year, she reached the finals of the U.S. Open. Venus drew attention as the first **unseeded** player to make it to the finals in nearly 40 years.

Serena came on the scene a few months later and beat two top-10 players in the Ameritech Cup. The sisters were moving up

Venus (l) and Serena at the Lipton Championship final

in the rankings. By the end of 1997, Venus was ranked 22, and Serena was ranked 99.

Venus and Serena became well known during the 1998 season. They played against each other for the first time as **professionals** in the Australian Open. Venus won the match. She also won her first Grand Slam event in mixed doubles at the Australian Open.

That year, Venus also set a record for the fastest serve in **Women's Tennis Association (WTA)** history.

Venus competes at the 1997 U.S. Open.

She hit a serve clocked at 127.4 miles per hour! Serena also won her first Grand Slam event in 1998. She won the mixed doubles tournament at Wimbledon. When the season ended, Venus was ranked number 6 and Serena was number 20.

THE MAKING OF AN AWESOME ATHLETE

Venus and Serena are among the top women's tennis players.

1980

Venus born June 17 in Lynwood, California

1981

Serena born September 26 in Saginaw, Michigan

1994

Venus turns pro

1995

Serena turns pro

Venus

How Awesome Are They?

See how Venus and Serena compare to other great tennis players on the WTA tour.

Player	Singles Titles	Doubles Titles	Grand Slam Titles
Jennifer Capriati	13	1	3
Kim Clijsters	12	7	0
Lindsay Davenport	38	33	6
Amelie Mauresmo	8	1	0
Serena Williams	**22**	**11**	**13**
Venus Williams	**29**	**10**	**12**

VENUS & SERENA

TOUR: WTA
RANK: Venus #3, Serena #1
YEARS PRO: Venus 8, Serena 7
HEIGHT: Venus 6'1", Serena 5'9"
WEIGHT: Venus 160, Serena 130

1997

Venus becomes the first unseeded player to make it to the U.S. Open finals in 40 years

2000

Venus and Serena win the Olympic gold medal in doubles

2001

Venus wins Wimbledon and the U.S. Open

2003

Serena beats Venus at the Australian Open to win the Grand Slam

Serena

- **In 1998, Venus set WTA fastest serve record of 127.4 mph**
- **In 1999, Venus and Serena were the first sisters to win a WTA event on the same day**
- **In 2001, Venus and Serena were the first sisters in 117 years to play against each other in the U.S. Open finals**

Highlights

Moving to the Top

In 1999, Venus and Serena broke another record when they became the first sisters to win a **WTA** event on the same day. Serena won her first singles title at the Gaz de France Open in Paris while Venus won the IGA Superthrift Tennis Classic in Oklahoma City, Oklahoma.

At the Lipton Championship, Venus beat Serena for the first time in a final. Fans were beginning to take interest in the **sibling** rivalry. They enjoyed watching the long-legged, hard-hitting girls play. But, they really enjoyed watching them play each other.

The girls paired together to win the French Open and U.S. Open doubles titles. But, the biggest thing to happen in the 1999 season was that Serena won the U.S. Open singles title. She beat Martina Hingis and became the first African-American woman to win a Grand Slam singles title since 1958. All along everyone expected Venus to win a Grand Slam first, but instead Serena pulled it off. By the end of the season, Venus was ranked number 3 and Serena was number 4.

Serena at the
1999 U.S. Open

The 2000 season started off slowly. Venus was sidelined with **tendinitis** in her wrists, and Serena was on a losing streak. Then, Serena was sidelined with tendinitis in her knee. But, both sisters were healthy and ready to play at Wimbledon. Venus won her first Grand Slam singles title, beating Lindsay Davenport in the final. The sisters also took home the doubles championship.

Venus kept the U.S. Open title in the family in 2000. She once again beat Davenport in the final. She had won Wimbledon and the U.S. Open in the same year. Both girls were selected to represent the United States in the summer Olympic Games in Sydney, Australia. They won the gold medal in doubles, and Venus brought home the gold medal in singles. Venus had an awesome year and was named Sportswoman of the Year by *Sports Illustrated.*

The 2001 season was also a good one for Venus. She won the women's singles event at Wimbledon and beat her sister in the finals at the U.S. Open. They became the first sisters in 117 years to play against each other in the finals at the U.S. Open. Venus and Serena also won the doubles championship at the Australian Open.

Venus (l) and Serena show off their Olympic gold medals.

Grand Slam

Just as 2000 and 2001 had belonged to Venus, 2002 was shaping up to be Serena's year. Even though Venus was ranked number 1 and Serena was ranked number 5, Serena quickly pulled ahead.

Serena beat Venus at the French Open. Then, she beat her again at Wimbledon for her second Grand Slam title in a row. The sisters then paired to defeat Virginia Ruano Pascual and Paola Suarez in the Wimbledon doubles championship.

The sisters met once again at the U.S. Open finals in 2002. Venus was the two time defending champion coming in. Serena beat Venus 6-4, 6-3 in the U.S. Open and proved to the world that she was indeed the best player in women's tennis.

Venus in action at the 2002 U.S. Open

Venus (l) and Serena pose with their trophies at the 2002 U.S. Open.

Serena had pulled ahead of her sister in the rankings and was now ranked number 1. Venus moved to the number 2 spot. Now it was on to the Australian Open, where Serena would be going for the Grand Slam of tennis.

Only four other women had ever held all four Grand Slam titles at the same time. Serena was determined to become the fifth. Once again, Venus and Serena were playing against one another in the final. This was the fourth

Serena competes in the 2003 Australian Open.

straight Grand Slam all-Williams final. The match was close, but when it was over Serena had won.

Serena became the holder of all four Grand Slam titles at the same time at the age of 21. This quickly became known as the "Serena Slam." The Williams sisters also won the doubles competition at the Australian Open in 2003. Serena still holds the number 1 ranking on the tour, while Venus has slipped to number 3.

Serena proudly holds her trophy
at the 2003 Australian Open.

Best Friends

While Venus and Serena are fierce competitors on the court, they are still best friends. Growing up, Serena always looked up to Venus. Whatever Venus did, Serena also wanted to do.

When Venus put beaded braids in her hair, Serena did the same. She ate the same foods Venus did, dressed like her, and talked liked her. It wasn't until Serena was 18 years old that she realized that she was different than Venus, that she had different likes and dislikes than her sister.

Serena enjoys acting and is pursuing an acting career. She loves designing clothes and will soon open her own clothing line. She also likes to surf and play the guitar. Venus has an interior design business, V Starr Interiors, that keeps her busy. She enjoys reading and watching movies.

Venus and Serena share a mansion in Palm Beach Gardens, Florida. Serena also has a condominium in Los Angeles and enjoys spending time with her two dogs, Jackie and Bambi. Venus has a dog named Bobby.

Venus and her sister Isha announce the launch of V Starr Interiors.

Venus and Serena have signed many **endorsement** deals, making them two of the highest-paid athletes of all time. Venus made $40 million in a deal with Reebok. Serena made $12 million in a deal with Puma. Serena also recently signed a $500,000 deal with Close-Up toothpaste to star in a commercial.

The Williams sisters are dominating women's tennis today. Their strength, speed, **agility**, and determination have brought these sisters from the crumbling courts in Compton to the top of the tennis world. They have become strong role models for many young women, and this is being recognized with awards off the court as well.

At the 34th **NAACP** Image Awards on March 13, 2003, Venus and Serena were presented with the President's Award. The Image Awards are held annually to celebrate the outstanding achievements of people of color. NAACP president and CEO, Kweisi Mfume, said that the sisters are "more than champions on the tennis courts, they are prime examples that there is no substitute for brains, hard work and dedication."

On May 20, 2003, Serena was honored as Sportswoman of the Year at the 2003 Laureus World Sports Awards.

How long will these sisters remain at the top? Only time will tell.

Venus (r) and Serena accept the President's Award at the 34th NAACP Image Awards.

Glossary

agile - to move with ease.

endorsement - allowing a company to use your name and image to sell a product in exchange for money.

National Association for the Advancement of Colored People (NAACP) - an American organization dedicated to upholding the civil and constitutional rights of African Americans.

professional - working for money rather than pleasure.

sanction - to approve or authorize.

sibling - a brother or sister.

tendinitis - an inflammation of the tendons.

unseeded - not part of a tournament ranking.

Women's Tennis Association (WTA) - a professional women's tennis tour that regulates competitions around the world.

Web Sites

To learn more about Venus and Serena Williams, visit ABDO
Publishing Company on the World Wide Web at
www.abdopub.com. Web sites about Venus and Serena
Williams are featured on our Book Links page. These links
are routinely monitored and updated to provide the most
current information available.

Index